W9-AUC-108

HORSE CARVING

WITH
TOM WOLFE

Text written with and photography by Douglas Congdon-Martin

Schiffer Publishing Ltd

77 Lower Valley Road, Atglen, PA 19310

Copyright © 1994 by Tom Wolfe
Library of Congress Catalog Number: 94-66377

All rights reserved. No part of this work may be reproduced
or used in any forms or by any means – graphic, electronic or
mechanical, including photocopying or information storage
and retrieval systems – without written permission from the
copyright holder.

Printed in Hong Kong
ISBN: 0-88740-649-1

We are interested in hearing from authors with book ideas on
related topics.

This book is meant only for personal home use and recreation.
It is not intended for commercial or manufacturing purposes.

Published by Schiffer Publishing Ltd.
77 Lower Valley Road
Atglen, PA 19310
Please write for a free catalog. This book may be pur-
chased from the publisher. Please include $2.95 postage.
Try your bookstore first.

Contents

Introduction

John W. Adams
Nov 1994

There is something almost magical about horses. They have a spirit that is contagious. This is particularly true of young colts, like the one we will carve in this book. As soon as they have their legs beneath them, they seem filled with the joy of life, frolicking in an unbridled dance. As they mature, the dance takes on more power and beauty, so it is little wonder that horses have a central place in the arts.

When I wrote a book called *Carving the Civil War* a few years ago, I was surprised how much response I got from the horse that was included in the gallery. I received hundreds of letters and phone calls asking for more patterns, and suggesting that I do a book concentrating on realistic horses. I had been carving them for years, and always enjoyed the work, but I never realized how popular they were.

This book is a response to those letters. I've carved one of those frisky colts included a pattern for its twin and its sire. There are also patterns for a work horse and a farm bred horse. The carving involves both knife work and power tools. The basic work is done with the knife, as it is in all my carvings. But for muscle tone and details like hair, the flexible shaft power tool and reversible rotary tool are wonderful. With the proper bits it can do things that are impossible with the knife, and bring great realism to the carvings.

I hope you enjoy this book and the carvings you make using it!

Carving the Horse

7½ wide
2 thick   7½ tall

Top Right: Cut the pattern out of a bass wood blank, 2" thick. I always buy wood in 4" thick pieces, so I can get two blanks out of one sawing. The grain should run up and down through the legs.

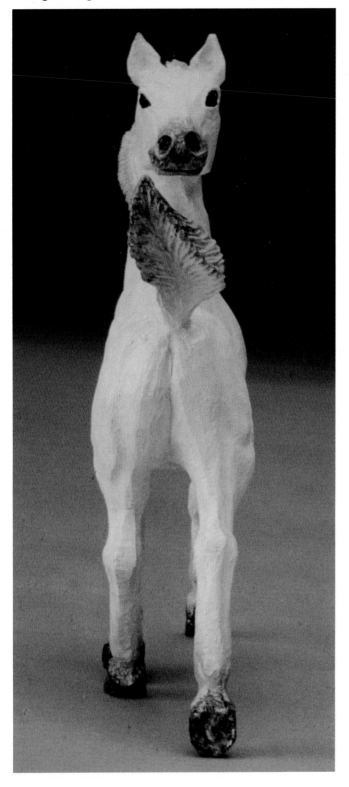

Center Right: Cut between the legs to separate them. Mark the legs to be removed and carve or drill them away...

Bottom Right: on both sides.

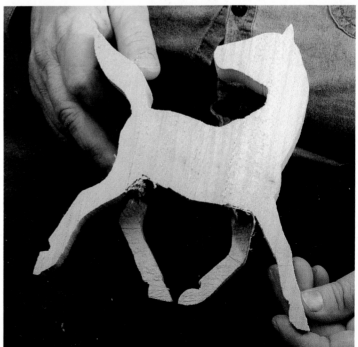

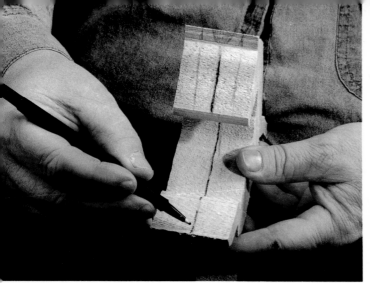

It's always a good idea to draw a center line all around. I use a pen for the camera's sake, but you're much better off using a pencil.

Mark the width of the tail at the body and flare it out to the end. I leave it wide at the end so I can do what I want with it later.

Mark the ears and the width of the head.

Start at the mane line and knock off the corner behind the head. Leave the mane intact.

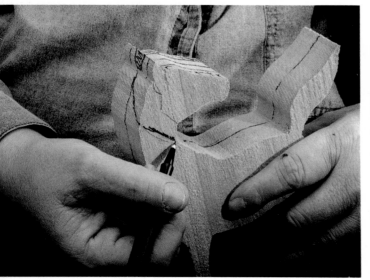

The hardest part of this carving is that the head is turning around. I begin by marking the spiral of the mane.

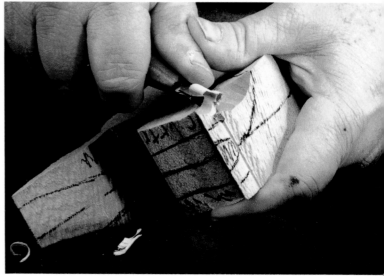

Be careful not to cut into the ear.

Again start at the mane and work to knock off the corner of the shoulder. Still leave the mane untouched.

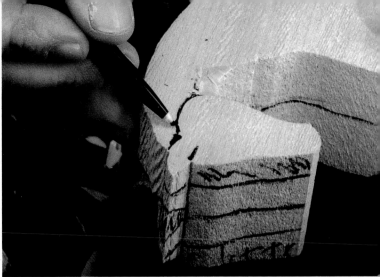

Mark the jaw and ear line on the other side of the head.

Continue the mane around to the nape.

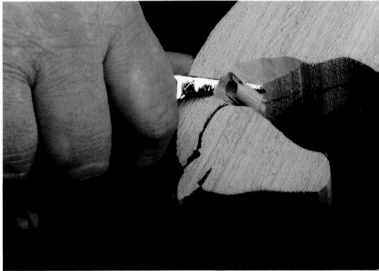

Cut a stop in the jaw line and come back to it from the neck.

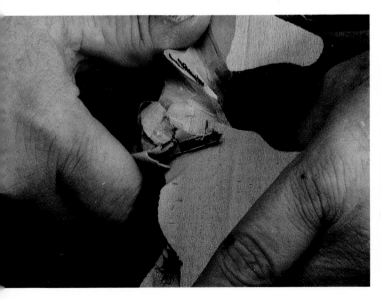

Thin the chest area.

Knock off the corner of the neck.

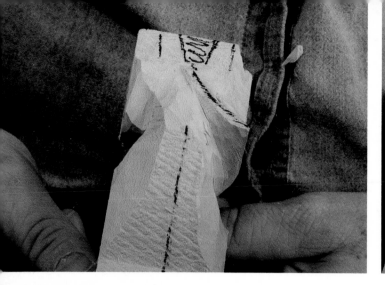

Progress on the neck.

Keep narrowing right on up the neck.

Bring the shoulder down. The tendency is to make shoulders of animals square, like human shoulders. Instead they are more as your shoulders would be if you took your hands together and pulled them way in front of your body.

Draw in the guzzle line on the underside of the neck.

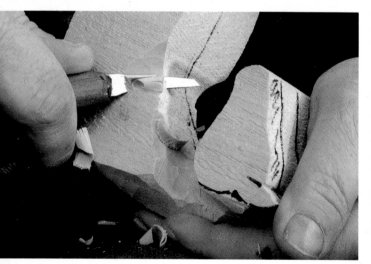

Repeat on the other side.

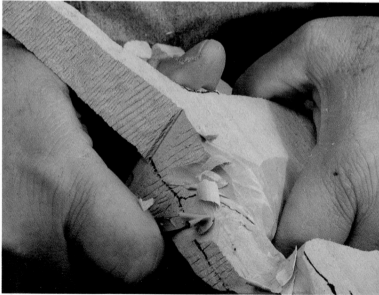

As you thin the neck, keep the line of the guzzle intact.

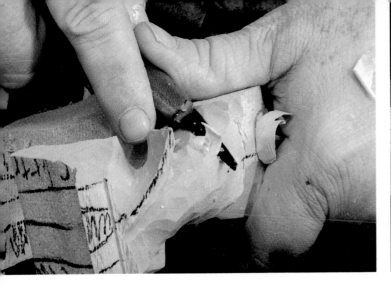

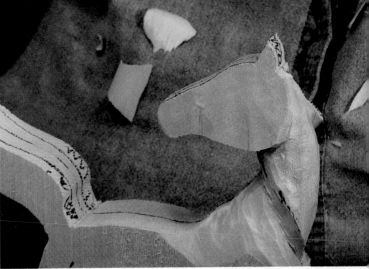

Go back and refine the neck. Most people have a tendency to leave the horse too thick, but in some places they are quite sleek.

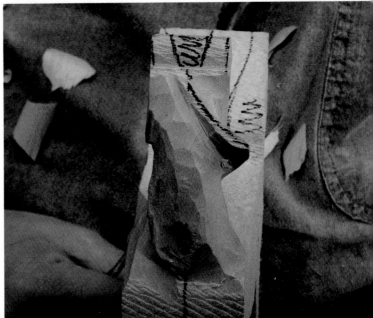

Pop off the sides of the head.

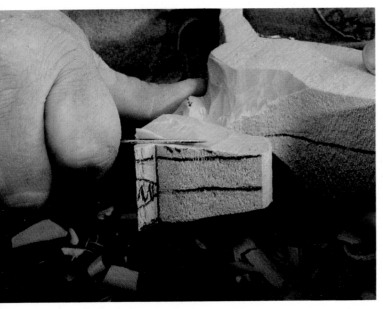

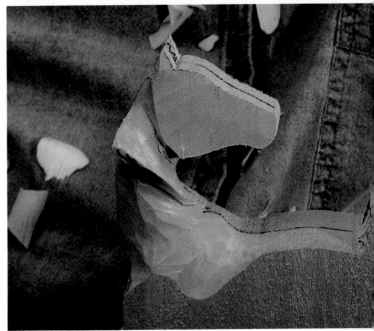

Repeat on the other side.

Progress on the head. A nice spiral is taking shape.

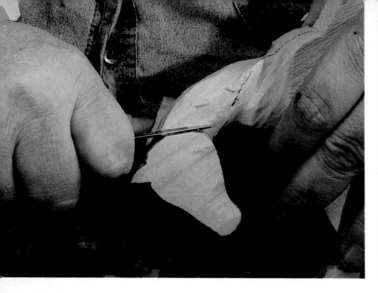

The neck needs a whole lot of thinning. Cut a stop in the jaw line...

Repeat on the other side.

and trim back to it. Continue this process until you reach a realistic thinness for the neck.

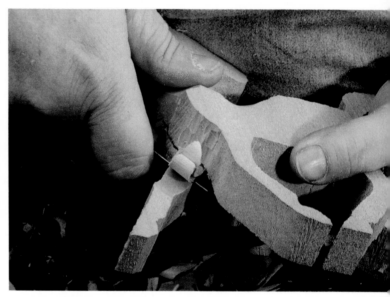

Open up a gap between the front legs by thinning the inside of the thighs.

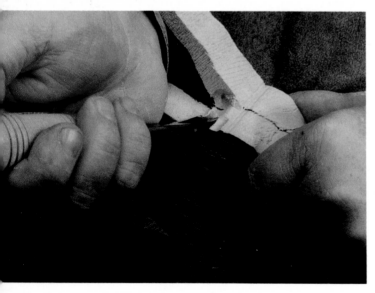

These marks on the front legs were left by the drill press when I removed the extra legs. I need to clean them.

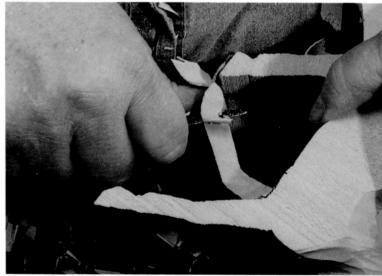

Thin the inside of the legs. The realistic horse does not have the knock-kneed look of a caricature horse.

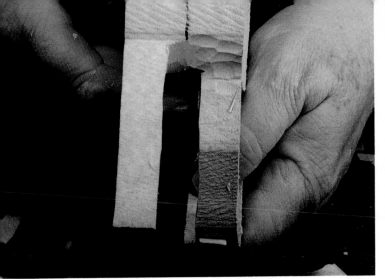

Thin the inside of the legs to about this point.

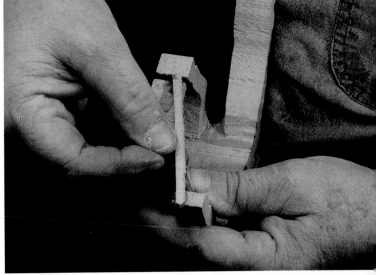

The leg grain is weak and will get weaker as they are thinned. Gluing braces to the feet should help stengthen them for carving. Keep the braces to the inside edge of the feet because you will be thinning the outside. Connect the front legs...

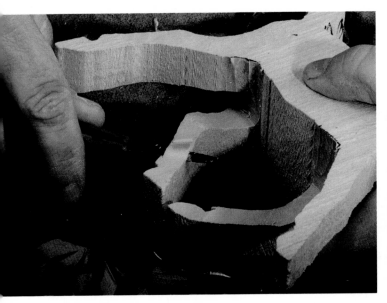

Repeat the process on the back legs. There isn't really an easy way to do this. You just need to work your knife through, then clean it up.

the back legs...

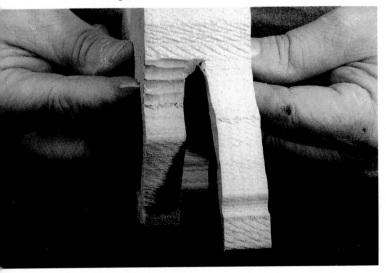

The gap between the back legs should be about the same as the front.

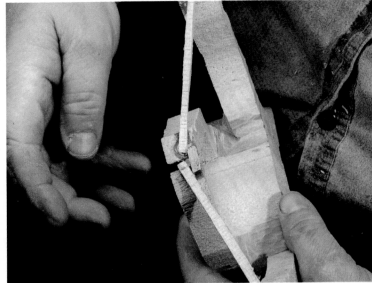

and between the two close legs, front and back.

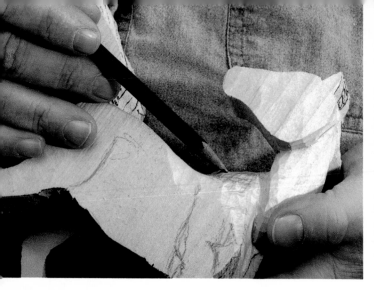

Refer to the pattern and mark the line of the legs on the flanks. Also mark any heavy areas like here above the shoulder. Mark it when you see it, or you are likely to have it there when you are finished.

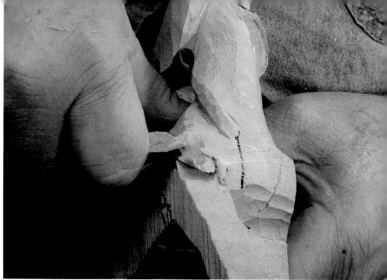

Trim the shoulder in front of the upper leg. Leave the muscle ridge that goes down to the breast.

Shorten the mane. If this were an adult horse I'd leave it and do something dramatic with it.

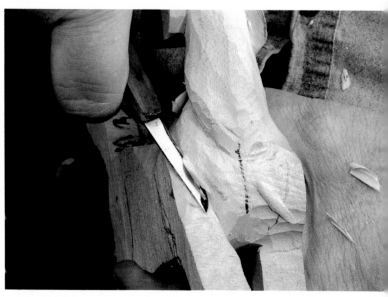

Define the line between the leg and the breast.

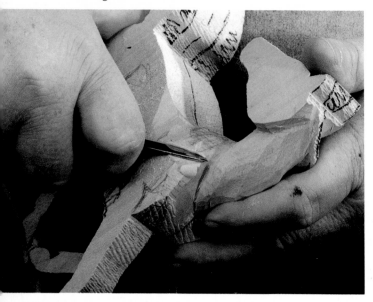

Clean up the shoulder, giving it more of a slope.

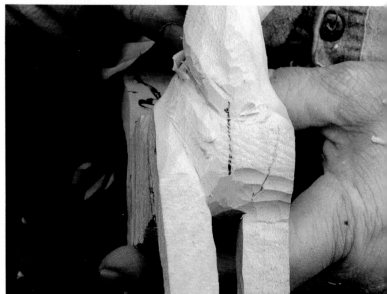

The result.

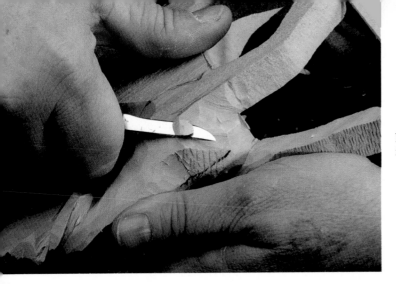

Do the other side the same way. Imagine that the line of the front of the leg continues right up to the shoulder.

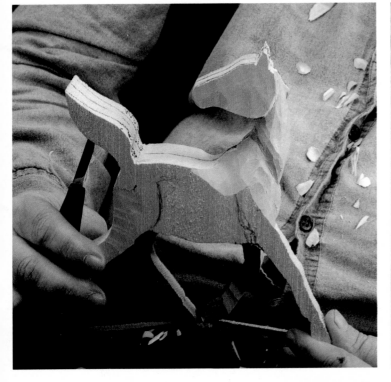
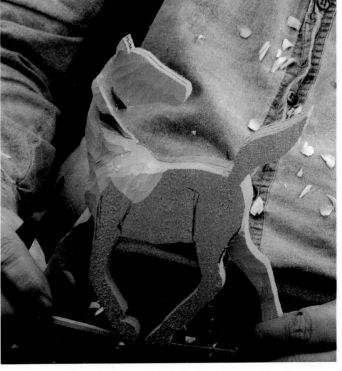

Progress.

Thin the tail by making a stop on the line of the rump...

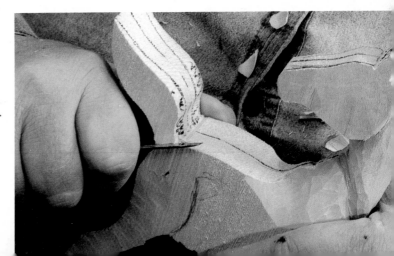

and trimming back to it. You want to leave the tail fairly thick right now for strength, but we need to shape the bottom so we can work on the rump.

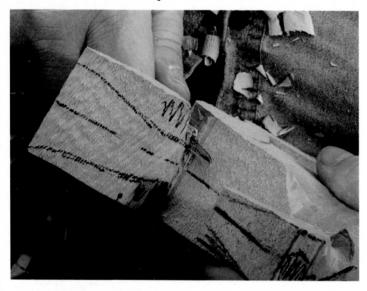

Do the other side the same way. The other advantage of leaving the top of the tail thick is that you still can do anything you want with it when you get to it.

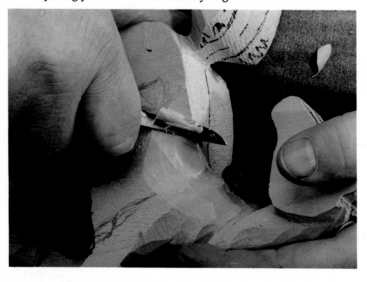

Knock off the corners of the back. Don't be afraid to make a fairly heavy cut here, otherwise it will have a squarish look.

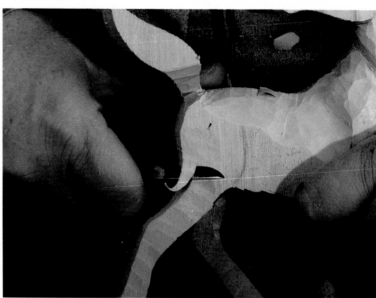

With the back rounded, come to the legs and round over the rump.

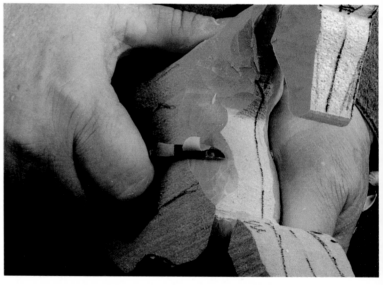

Repeat on the other side.

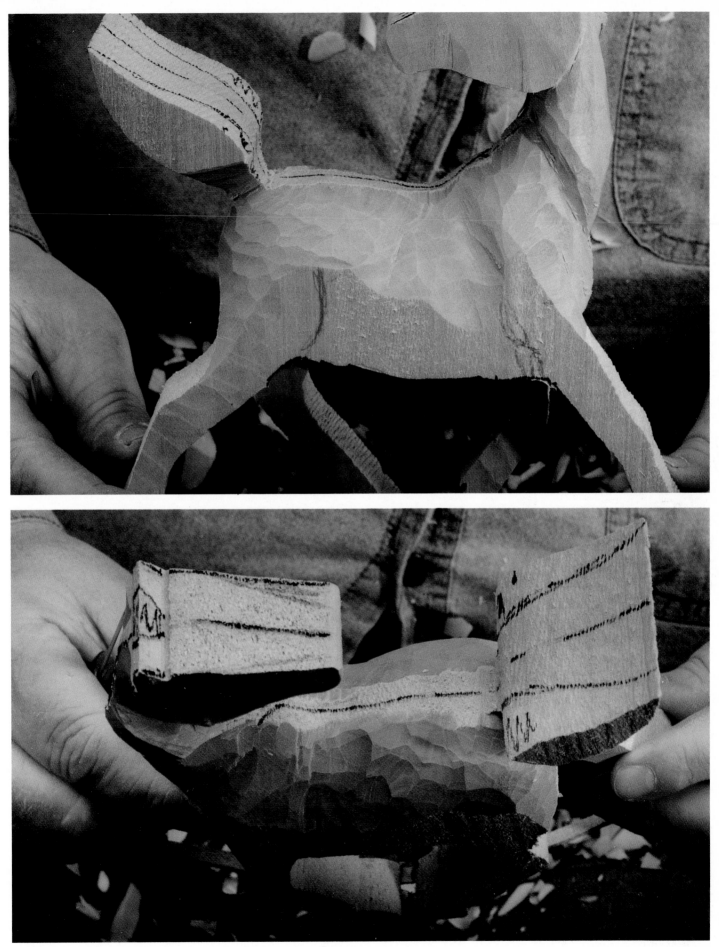

Progress.

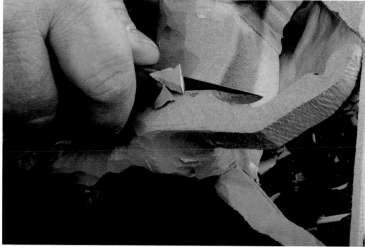

Begin to shape the belly by cutting a stop along the line of the leg. This needs to be good and square, going straight into the line.

and cut back to it.

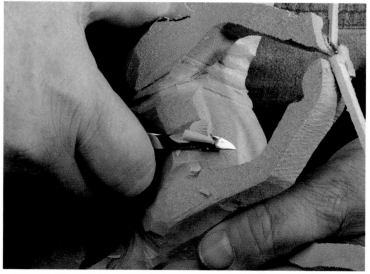

Trim back to it from the belly.

Knock off the corner of the belly.

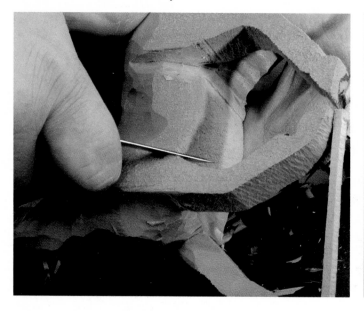

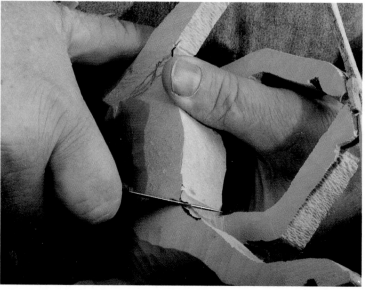

You can see here how far to trim at the back leg. Repeat on the front, a straight stop...

Repeat the process on the other side.

Progress.

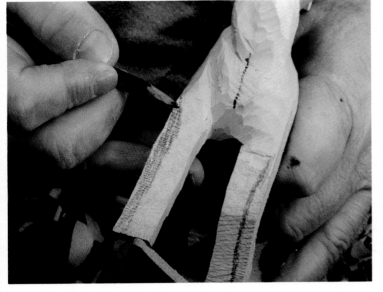

Draw in the outside of the legs to be removed. A colt's legs are rather spindly.

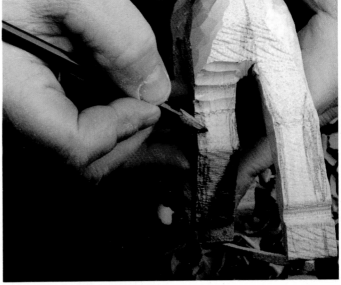

Do the same in the back. Here we also need to take a little bit more off the inside of the legs.

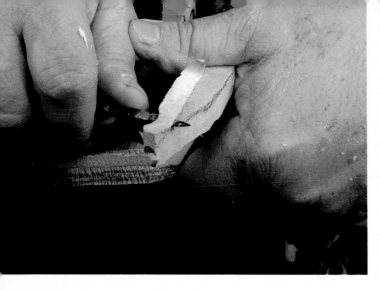

Cut off the excess, being sure to keep the legs square for now.

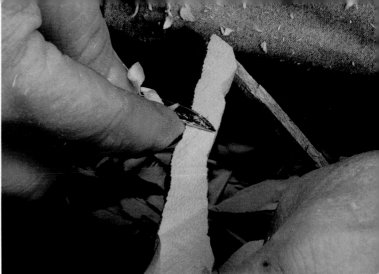

The shin is round, so one dimension needs to match the other. Use the knife blade to check this out, measuring one way...

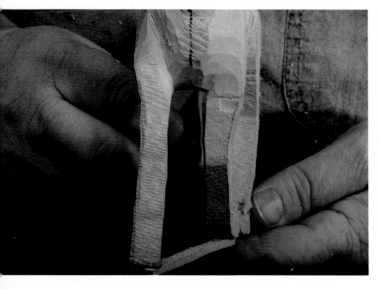

Starting to look like a colt's legs.

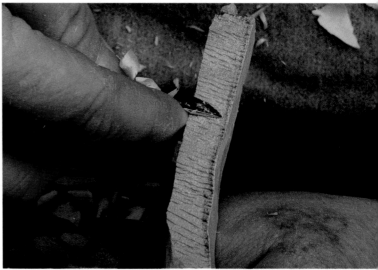

then the other. I need to remove a little from the side. Leave the knee joint heavy.

The inside of the back legs is not easy to get to, but a long-handled knife makes it easier.

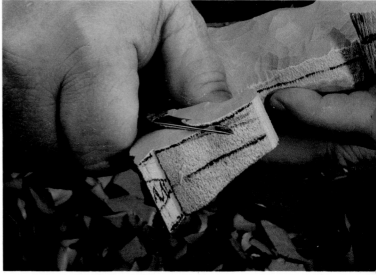

Thin the head toward the muzzle.

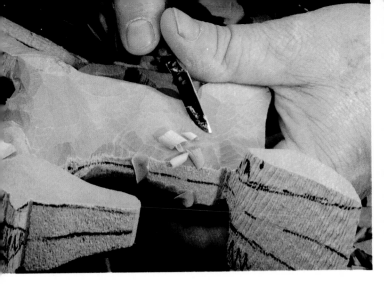

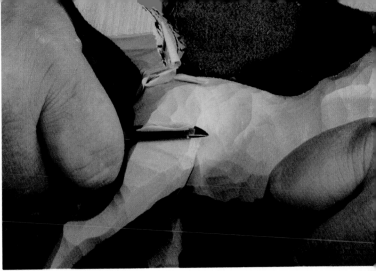

Go over the whole piece looking for places that need refinement. Trust your eyes. If it doesn't look right, it probably isn't.

The hips need to be a little thinner, and more sloping than square.

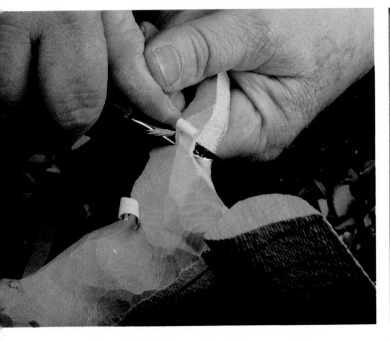

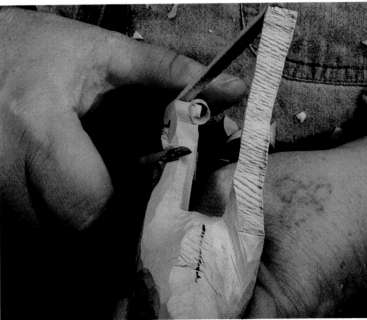

Knock the corners off the legs, taking them to octagon.

Repeat the process on the front legs, remembering to leave the knee joints heavy for now.

Continue to the hoof. The best way to get to round is to start square, go to octagon, then to round.

Find the narrowest hoof. Square the others to the same width.

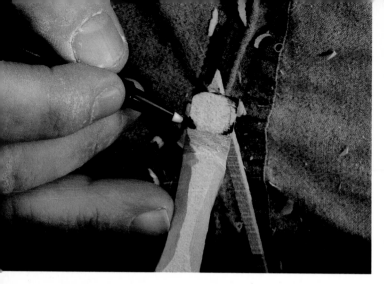

Mark the corners to be knocked off.

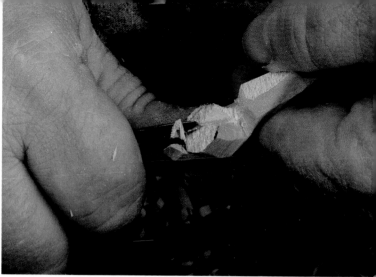

for this result.

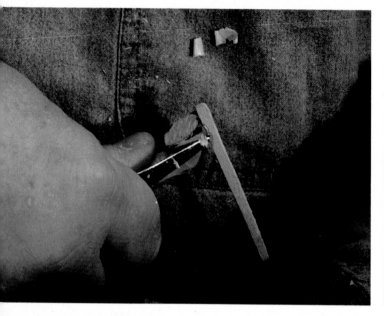

Knock the corners off.

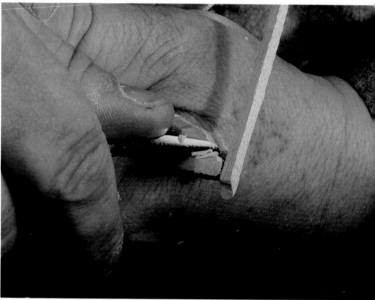

Knock the corners off the top of the hoof.

Cut the nitch of the frog at the back of the hoof...

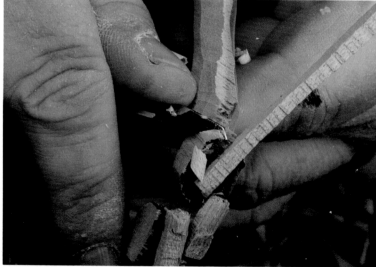

Repeat on the other hooves, doing as much as you can without weakening the brace. You can come back and finish after the brace is removed.

Now it's time to go back and knock off the corners of the octagon, taking things to round.

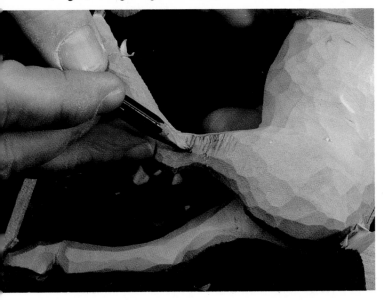

I've noticed that this area is thick, but I don't want to fix it now. To remember, I'll mark to make sure I come back after I round the edges.

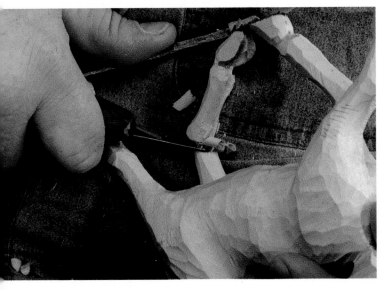

Continue rounding the legs.

Mark the tail. I've decided to put a little swirl in it.

Trim the tail.

Progress.

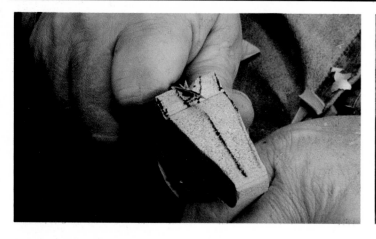

Clean between the ears.

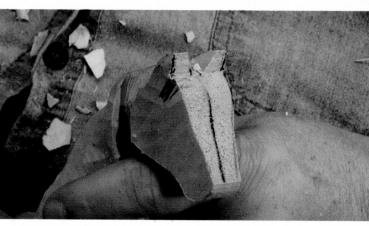

Carry the line of the ear down the head and mark the area of the forehead to be removed.

Take them to square.

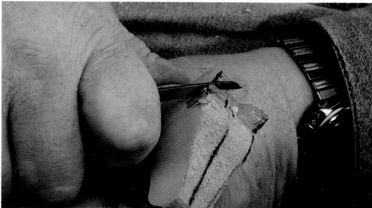

Cut a stop in the line of the ear and trim back to it from the forehead.

The result.

and one up.

The ears need to come in at the base.

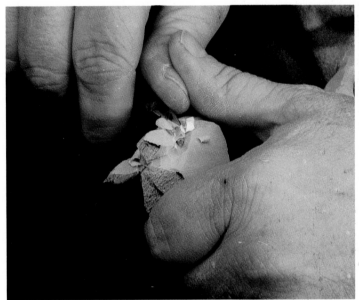

Continue to shape the ears and head...

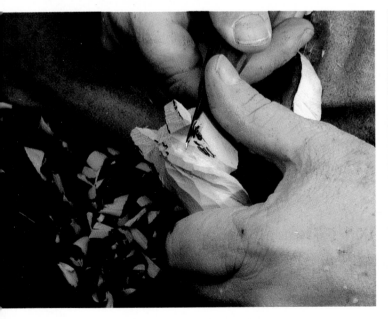

Take this off with two cuts, one down the ear...

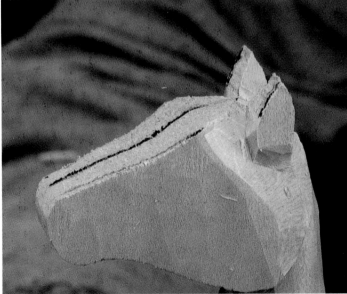

to this point from the side...

and the back.

Progress.

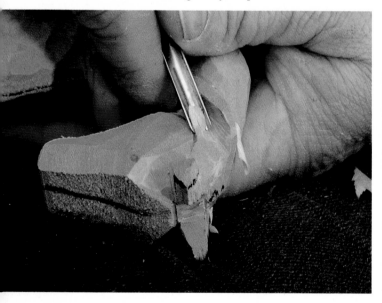

Take the cheek down, leaving the eye to protrude over it.

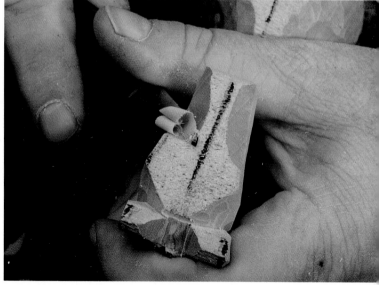

Knock the corner off the muzzle, leaving the eye socket.

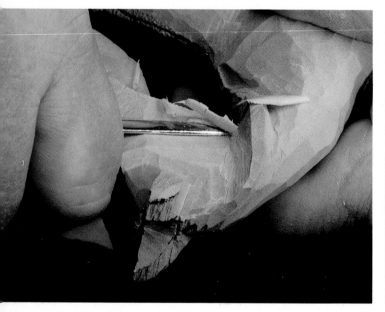

Redraw the outline of the jaw and come with a gouge behind the line.

The eyesocket protrudes over the muzzle.

Before proceeding, draw in the mane on the forehead.

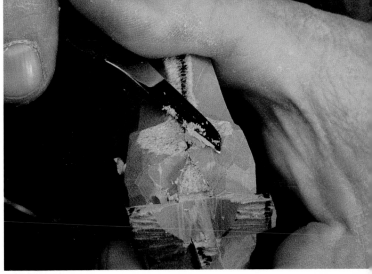

A little groove runs around the back of the eye, lifting it up. Make it with the knife, using a curl cut.

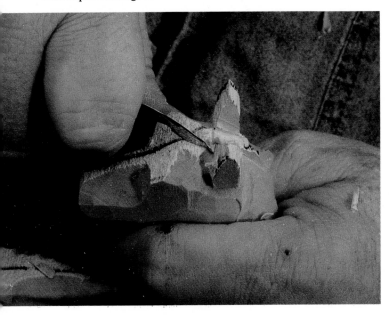

Cut a stop in the line of the mane...

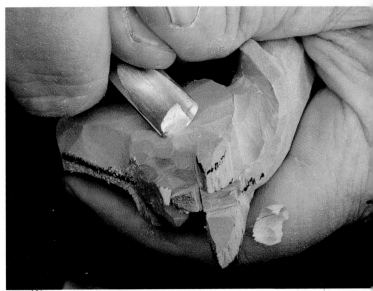

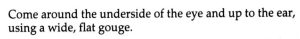

Come around the underside of the eye and up to the ear, using a wide, flat gouge.

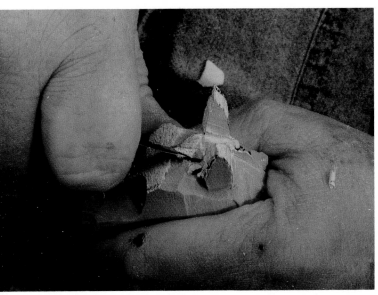

and trim back to it from the forehead.

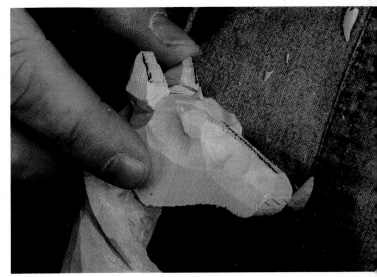

The result.

There is a another curve between the cheek and the mouth.

Draw in the mouth...

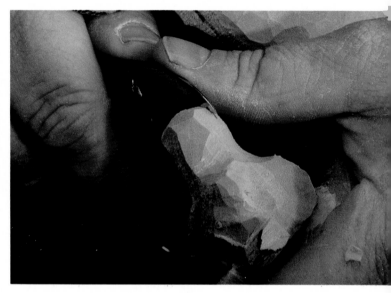

and cut a stop in the line.

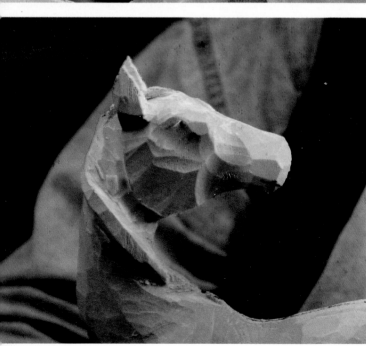

Progress on the head.

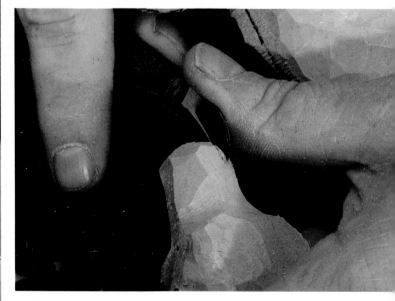

Cut back to it from the bottom lip, making it look as though the bottom lip is coming under the top lip.

Come into the corners of the mouth with a veiner...

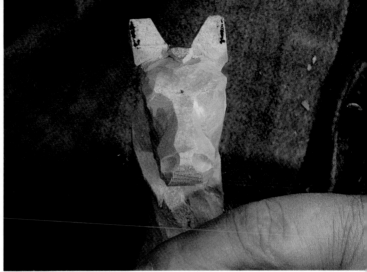

for this result. The colt is playful, and its nostrils are flaring.

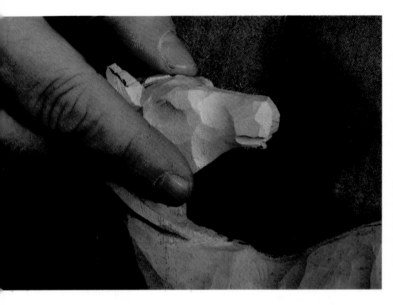

for this result.

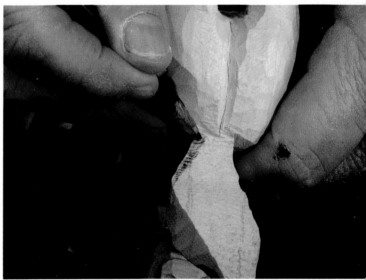

We need to narrow the base of the tail.

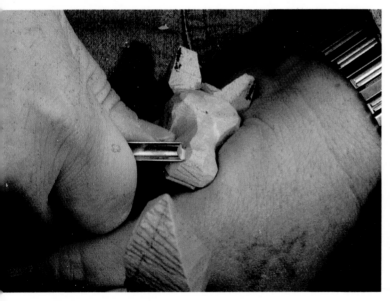

Gouge out the nostrils...

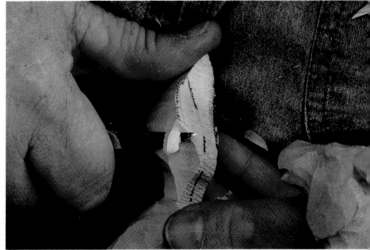

Trim the marked area then knock the corner off the top of the tail. Notice all the fingers I am using to support the tail. This is cutting across the grain, and bracing is necessary to avoid breakage.

Continue on the other top edge.

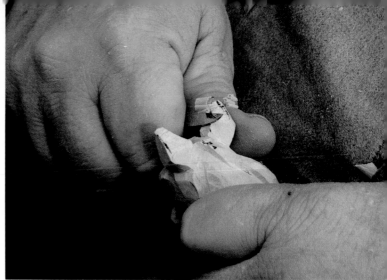

Returning to the head, I'm going to shape the ears a little better.

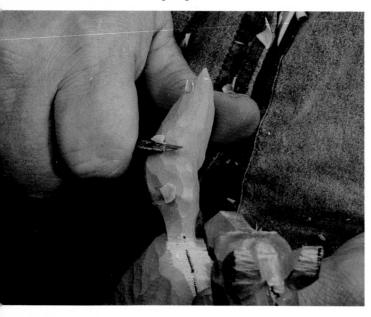

Round over the top of the tail.

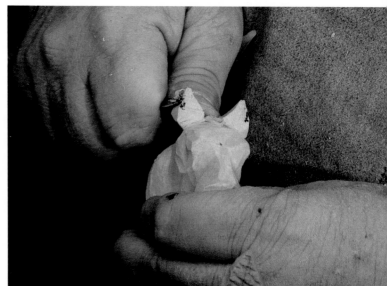

I need to toe-in the outside surface.

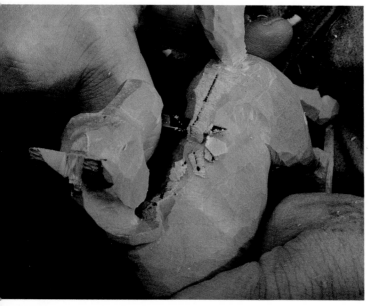

While I'm here I'll clean up the marks on the back.

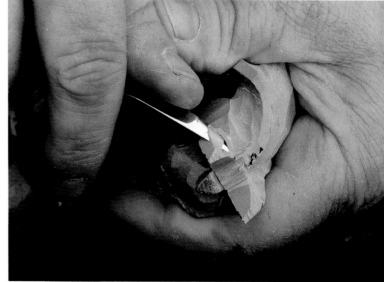

Knock off the back corners. The ears are going to be perked forward, which in this cased is perked forward backwards.

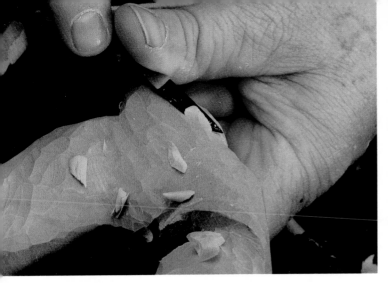

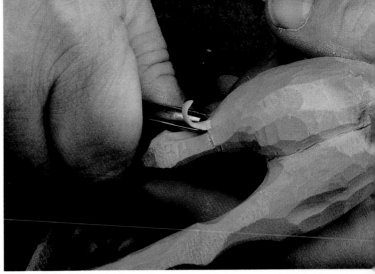

Before moving to the power detail I go over the whole piece to refine and smooth the surface. I'm looking for bumpy places or areas that need to be reduced.

With a gouge cut some of the leaders that come down the back of the leg.

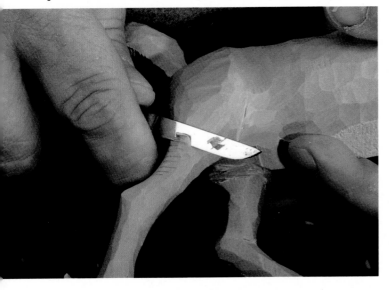

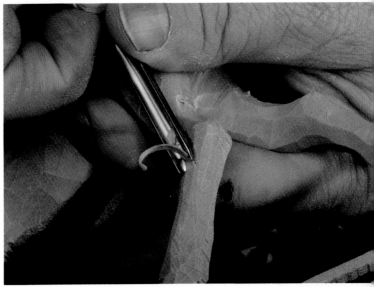

These marks remind me to thin the upper leg here.

These continue down into the lower leg...

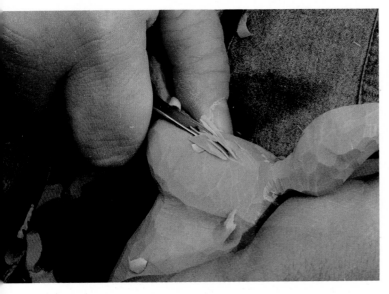

There is a muscle that comes up the flank. I'll start it with the knife, using a curl cut, and finish it with a detailer. Repeat on the other side.

like this.

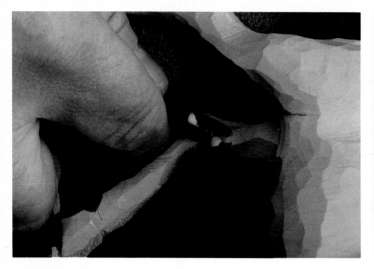

They are on the inside as well as the outside.

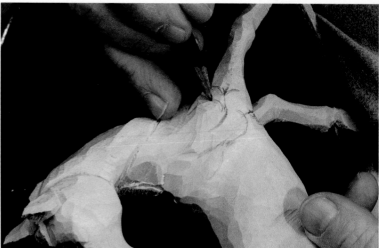

Draw in the muscle patterns.

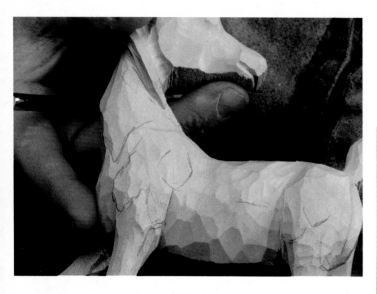

Here you see how they could look on the left...

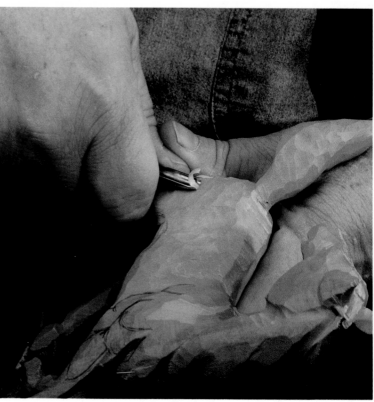

Run down the lines with a half-round gouge.

and the right.

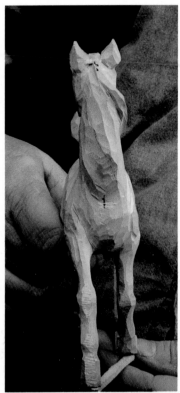

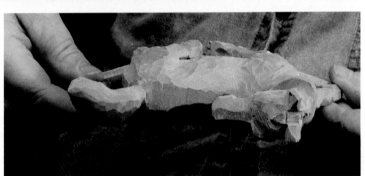

Ready for detailing.

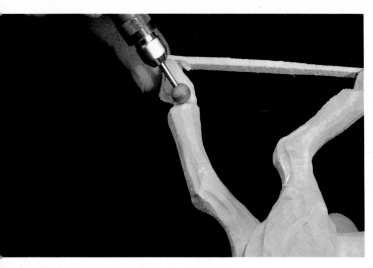

Go around the shank with a ruby ball.

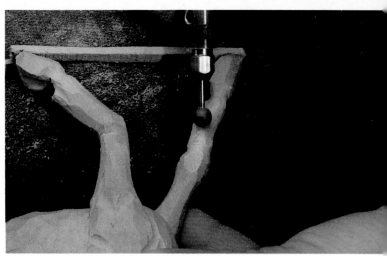

The forward leg is the smallest of the group, so I'll begin by dressing it down. This allows me to bring all the legs to about the same size.

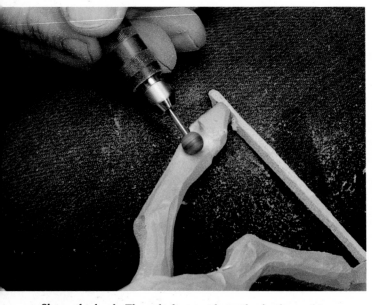

Shape the hock. The colt does not have the feathers a big draft horse would have.

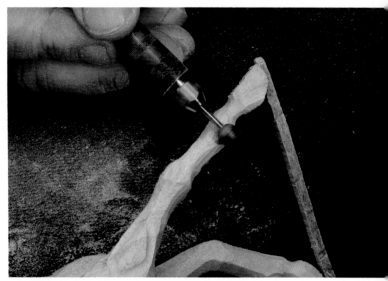

Doing this work with short strokes leaves a hair texture at the same time.

Continue with shanks and hocks on the other three legs.

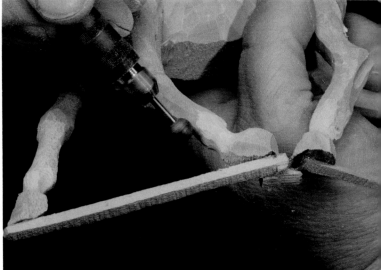

With the shank carved to the size I want it I move to the next leg and make it match.

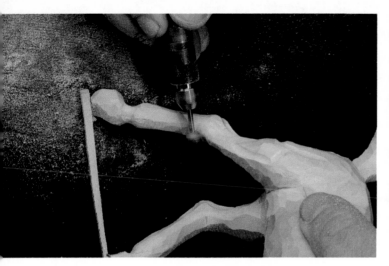

The back legs will be a little bigger than the front. I start with the smaller of the two and begin thinning down the thick spots.

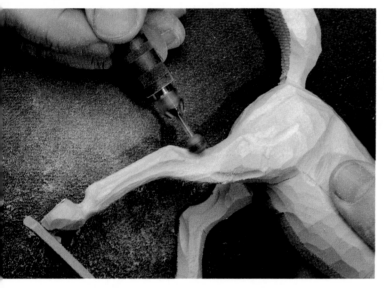

You don't want to lose the lines of the leaders that you started with the gouge.

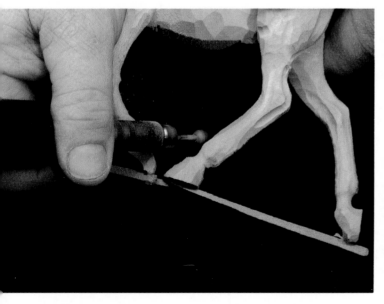

When one back leg is established shape the other to match.

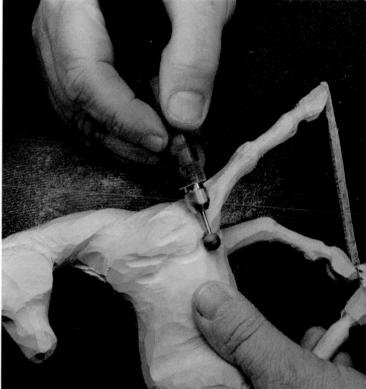

When the lower legs are complete, continue above the knees. Keep the muscle shapes you established earlier.

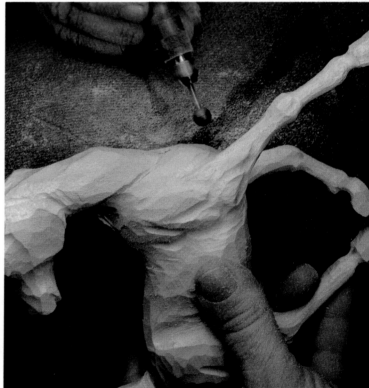

It's just a matter of refining things as you go.

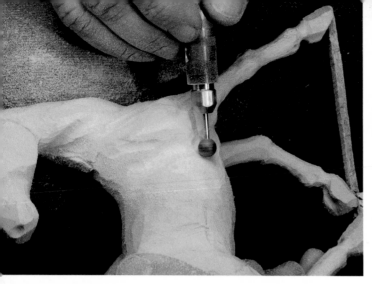

Some high places can be smoothed out with this tool, and some are better done with a knife.

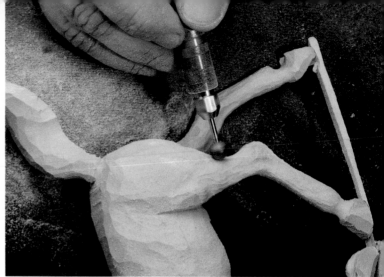

Blend and accentuate the muscle shapes you created with the gouge.

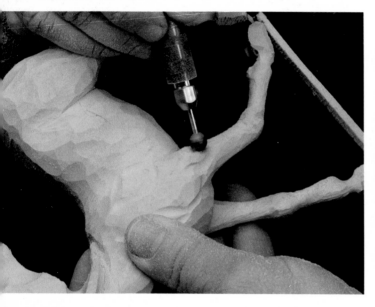

Continue with the other legs. The main thing here is getting them all to the same size.

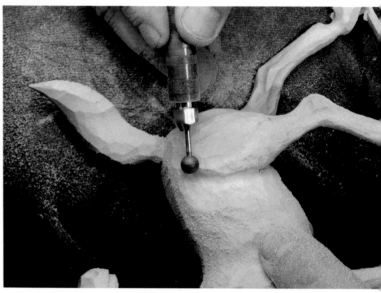

As you do the back legs, continue with the muscles of the rump.

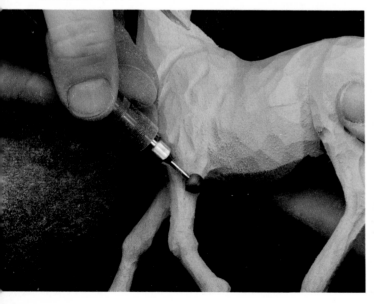

Bring out the elbow at the back of the upper front leg.

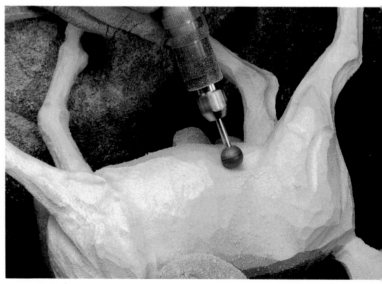

There is a fold here that connects the front of the back legs to the belly.

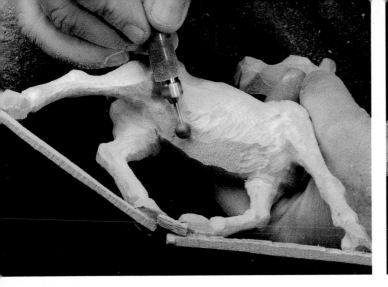

Shape the belly.

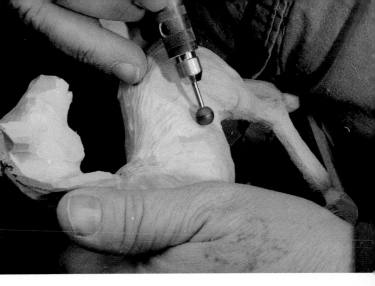

Continue to refine.

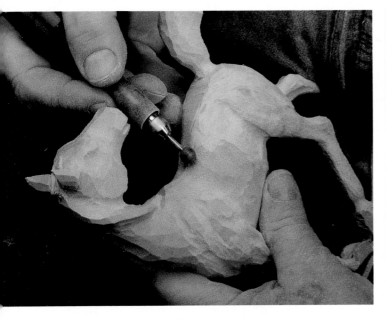

Moving to the back, you always want the strokes of the detailer to follow the line of the hair. When you are done shaping you will have much of the hair defined.

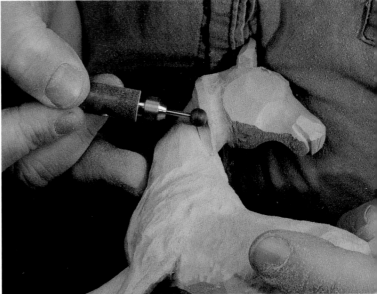

Narrow the mane. The colt's mane is pretty sparse, because it takes a while to grow.

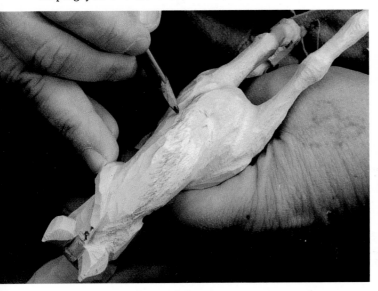

Mark areas that will be contoured.

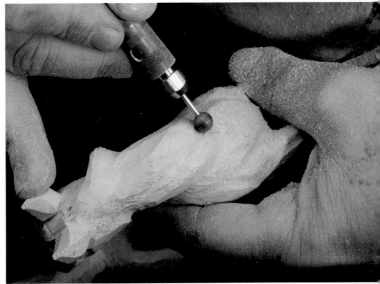

Cut the groove you marked in the neck.

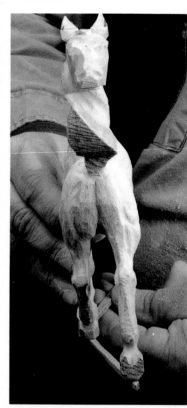

Progress report. Take special note of the neck. This head position puts a lot of strain on the neck muscles so they should be quite prominent.

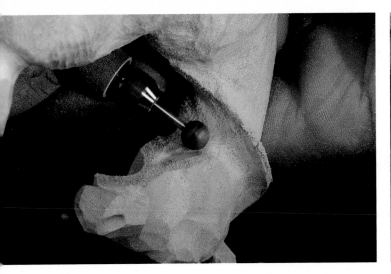

Work under the jaw to create the groove between the jawbones.

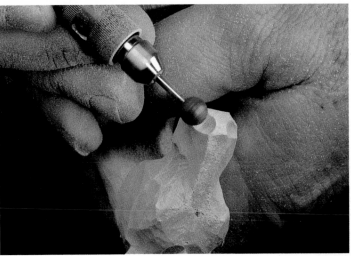

Deepen the nostrils.

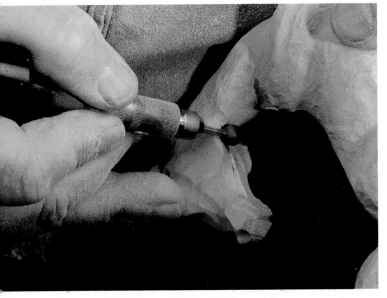

Still on the underside, create a groove along both edges from the muzzle to the back of the jaw. this leaves a waddle hanging down the center, lower than the jaw.

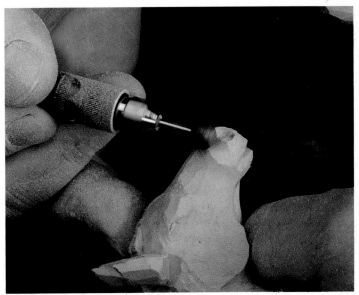

Cut a shallow groove betwen the lip and the nostril, carrying it around to the side.

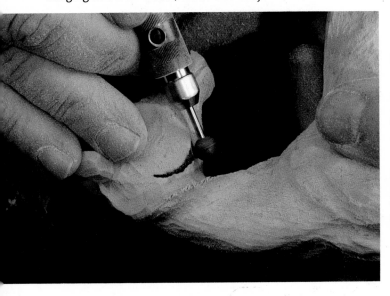

We need to thin and round the jaw.

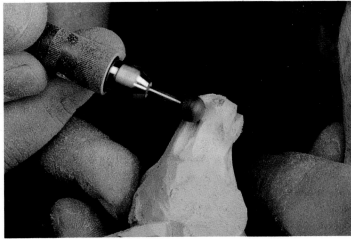

A groove runs along the top edge of the muzzle from the nose to the eye. This is particularly prominent on Arabians, flaring as they breathe. It has led to their nickname "Drinkers of the wind."

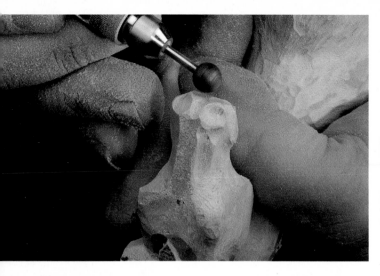

Cut a groove between the nostrils, carrying it around to the underside of the the front. This makes it flare out real good.

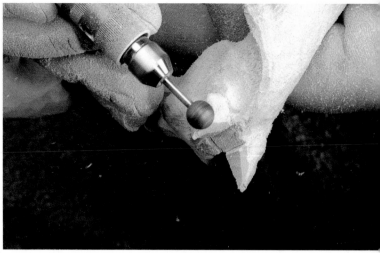

Blend from the ball up to the tip of the ear.

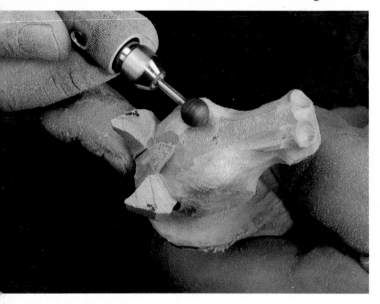

Shape the bulges of the eyes. They should be prominent, but more important than the size even is that they be equal. This prominent eye socket gives the horse almost peripheral vision, because the eye can pivot quite widely.

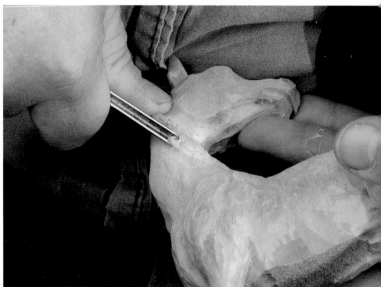

Thin and define the mane using a veiner.

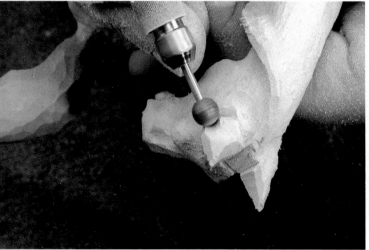

Begin shaping the ear by creating a ball at the base in the back.

While you are using the veiner, define the line between the hoof and the hair of the foot.

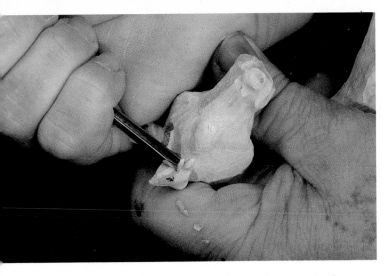

Open up the ear a little, creating a slot for the rotary tool.

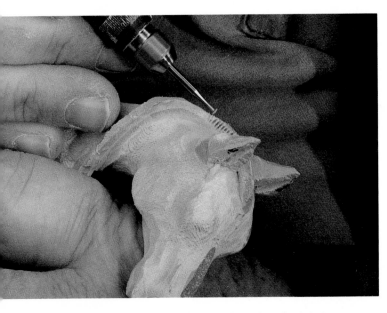

Create the hair of the mane using a little diamond disk.

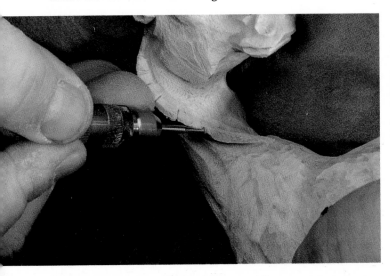

I first mark the angle of the hair every 1/4" or so, so I get it going the way I want it. Repeat on the other side, making sure the hair runs in more or less the same direction.

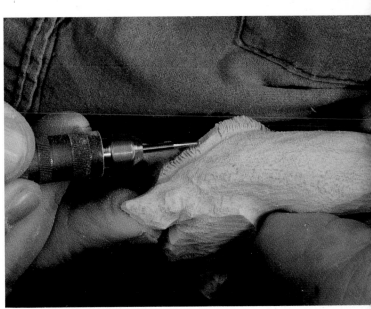

Use the diamond disk to fill in the hairs of the mane.

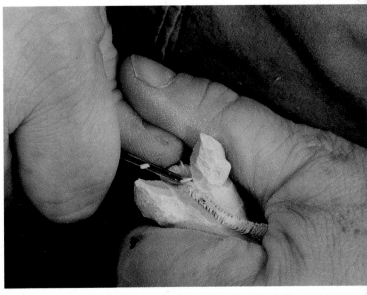

I use a veiner to add hair to the forelock, tying it in with the mane. A colt usually has more hair up here than on the mane.

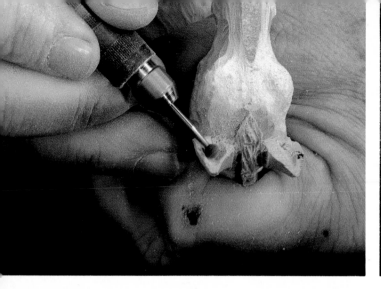

Switch to a small diamond ball bit to work around the ears.

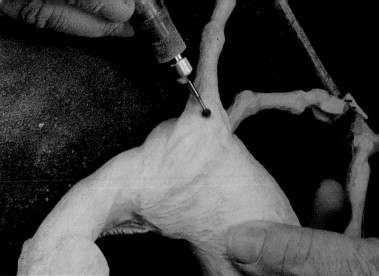

Go over the whole body. This tool is nice because it can be used both to accentuate lines, giving the piece drama and character, and to smooth lines, making it look realistic.

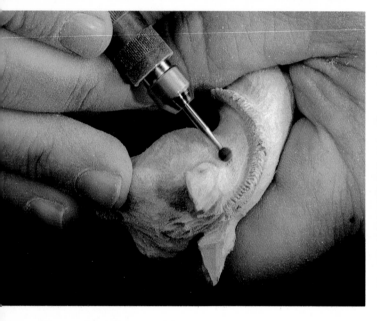

Deepen the definition of the outside of the ear, blending it into the head.

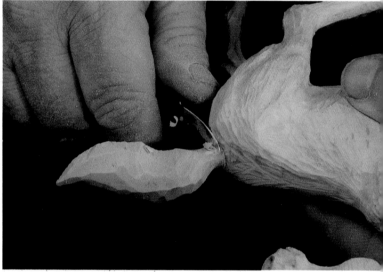

Move to the tail, narrowing the base to the size you want.

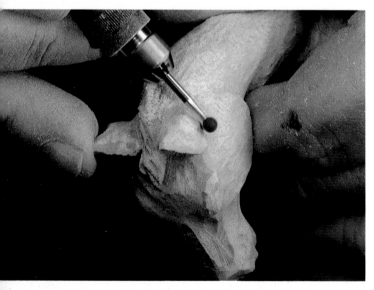

The diamond bit refines the lines made earlier by the larger ball, and makes smoother hair lines.

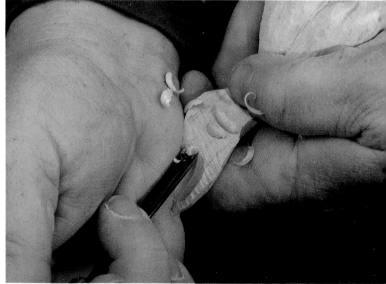

Cup the underside of the tail with the gouge...

for this result. No, this is not a self-portrait.

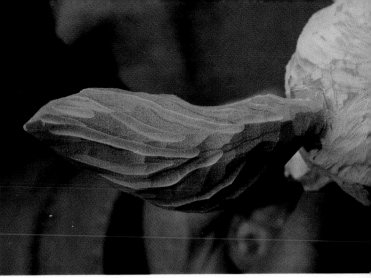

The major lines in place.

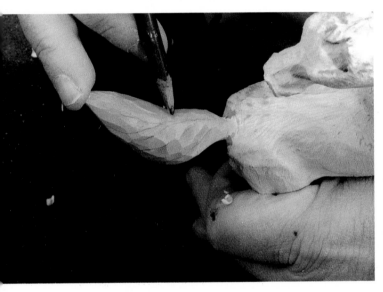

Draw in the basic movement of the tail.

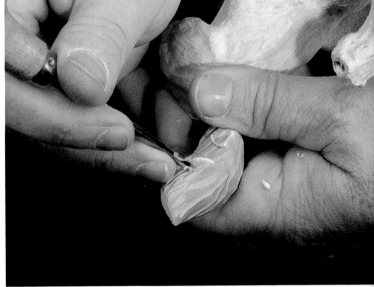

With a smaller veiner add the finer lines. These lines can go from line to line, but they can't go through a line. That would give the tail a checkered look.

The result.

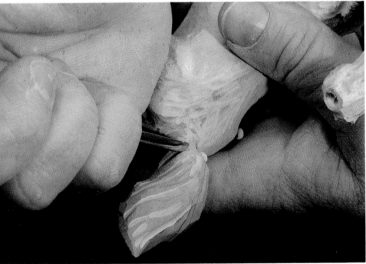

Establish the main lines with a gouge, generally following the lines you have drawn. Don't carry these heavy lines down to the base of the tail, which is much finer.

Continue with the hair on the underside of the tail.

The result.

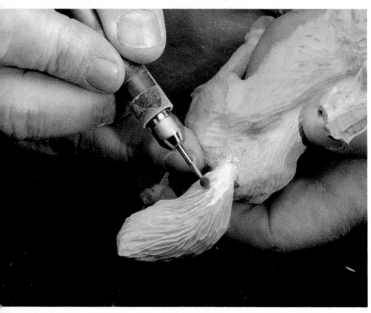

Use the diamond ball to trim up the tail and blend the hair.

It's time to remove the braces. Trim down to the glue, but not into it, with the knife. The epoxy will dull the knife.

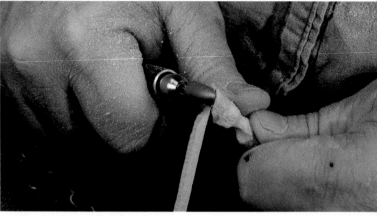

Finish the job with a rotary tool.

When the braces are off clean up the hoofs.

Switch to a cylinder shaped bit with a safe end on it to smooth the hoof. Carry the surface of the hoof to the hairline and make it smooth. When working on these fragile legs, be sure to hold the leg for strength.

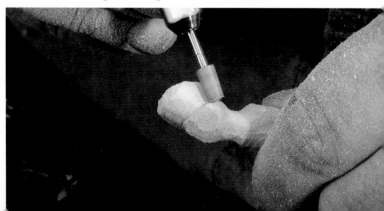

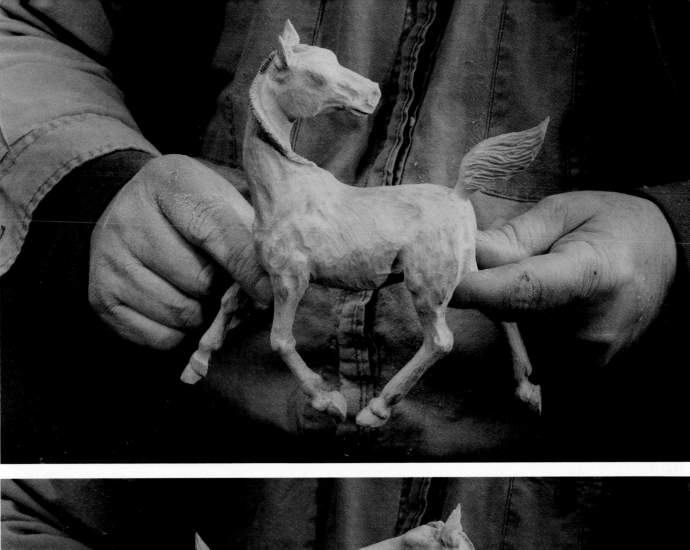

Ready for eyes.

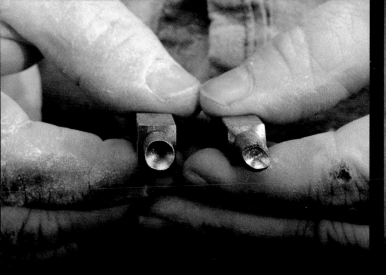

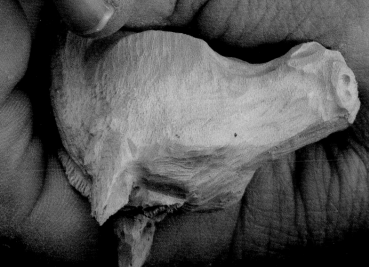

For the eyes I use an oval eyepunch. This is made from a round eyepunch with the sides ground down.

The eye runs almost on a line from the nose to the ear.

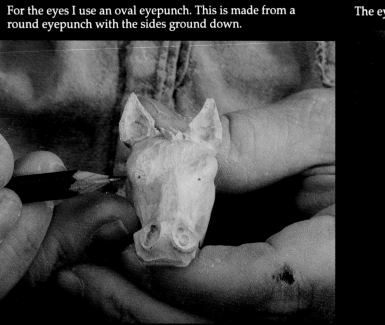

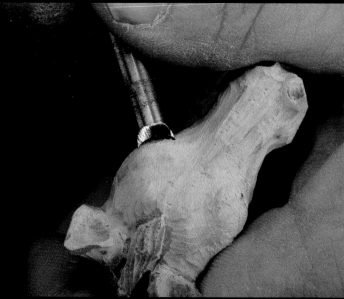

Mark the front corners of the eye so they are even.

Align the eyepunch with the front corner and push in on the lower edge...

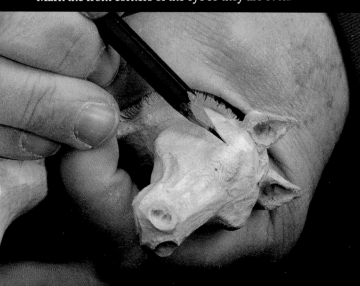

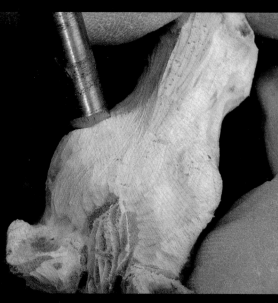

Mark the back corner.

the upper edge...

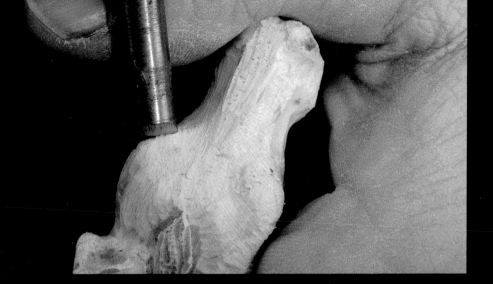

the front...

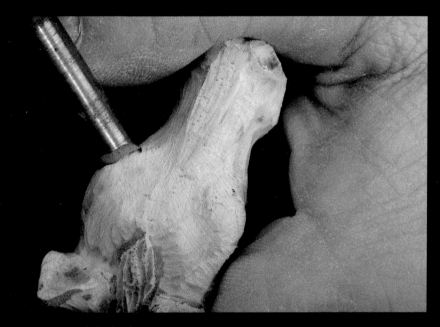

and the back. Repeat as necessary.

The result.

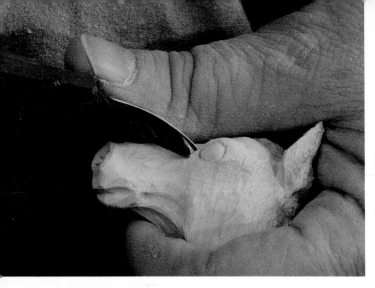

At the front corner of the eye make three cuts. First cut along the top eyelid...

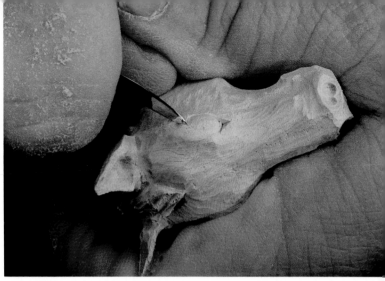

Repeat at the back of the eye...

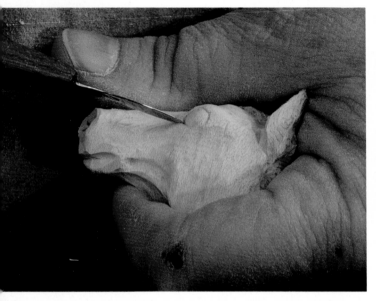

then along the bottom.

for this result. Follow the same steps on the other eye.

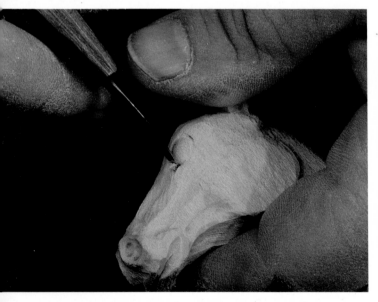

With the blade flat against the eye come into the corner to pop out the nitch.

Refine the eye by cutting stops along the lines made by the punch...

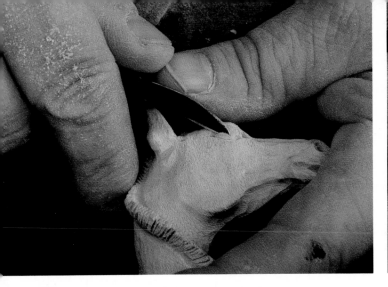

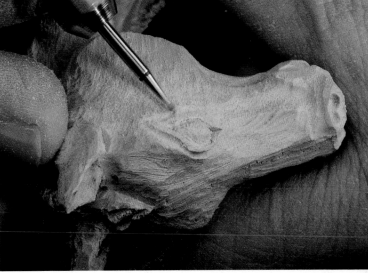

and coming back to them from the eyeball. This deepens the eye.

then the bottom.

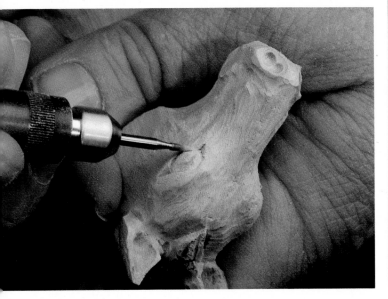

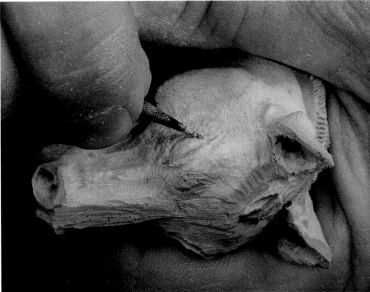

Use a pointed diamond bit to reshape the eyes, giving them the rounded shape the knife took away.

I sometimes use a bit without the rotary tool as a little rasp to clean out some tight spaces.

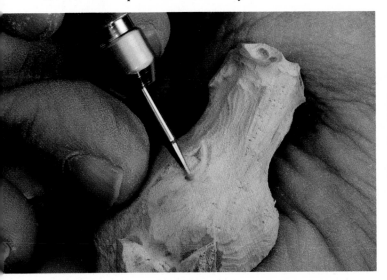

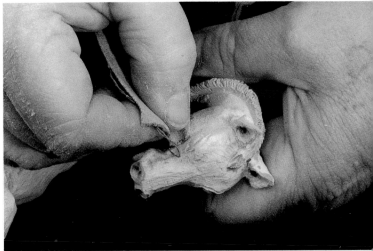

Switch to a small round diamond bit to create the eyelids. This is started by created a groove parallel to the eye opening. Do the top first...

A light sanding will take away the fuzzies. This is especially helpful on the head where it should be smooth. It's hard to get the skin-over-bone look the horse head has, but that is what you strive for.

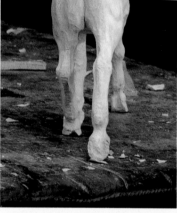

Ready for painting.

Painting the Horse

For wood carving I use Winsor and Newton Alkyd tube paints. Most coats are thinned with pure turpentine to a consistency that is soaked into the carving, giving subtle colors. What I look for is a watery mixture, almost like a wash. In this way the turpentine will carry the pigment into the wood, giving the stained look I like. It has always been my theory that if you are going to cover the wood, why use wood in the first place. It should be noted that with white, the concentration of the pigment should be a little stronger.

I mix my paints in juice bottles, putting in a bit of paint and adding turpentine. I don't use exact measurements. Instead I use trial and error, adding a bit of paint or a bit of turpentine until I get the thickness I want.

The juice bottles are handy for holding your paints. They are reclosable, easy to shake, and have the added advantage of leaving a concentrated amount of color on the inside of the lid and the sides of the bottle which can be used when more intense color is needed.

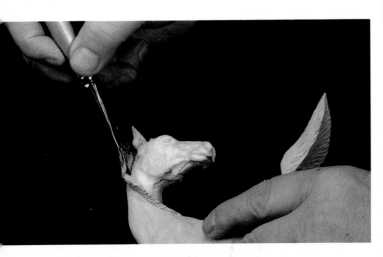

You can choose any paint combination you want. This horse is going with its twin and father in a set up, so I'm going to paint it white with brown highlights. Give the horse a wash of white. This will soak in real good.

The white applied. Let it dry before moving to the next step.

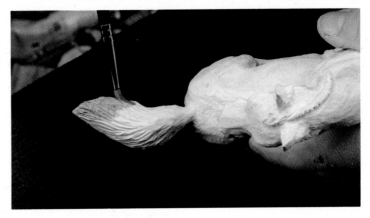

Follow the wash with a thick white paint. Applied after the wash has soaked in, this gives good coverage.

Next we apply a fairly thick mixture of raw sienna to the tail.

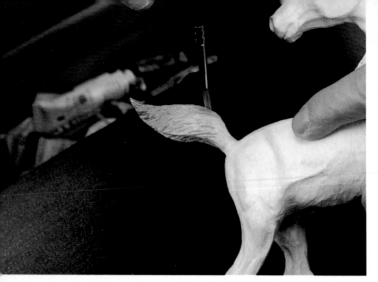

Let it fade into the white.

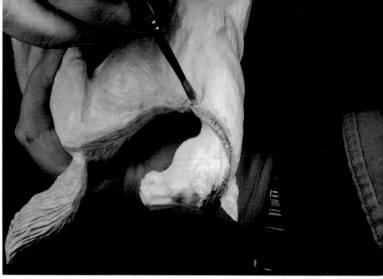

Dapple it into the white of the neck.

Do the same on the mane.

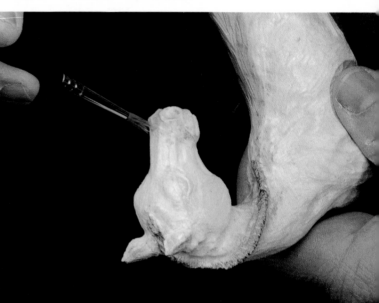

Dry the brush on a paper towel and dab the nose so the raw sienna is applied as freckles.

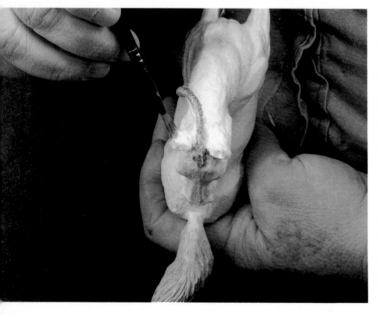

Apply it to the extremities and dry brush it out.

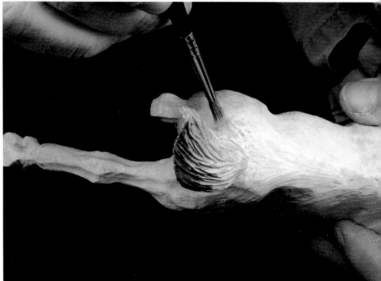

Do the same on the rump.

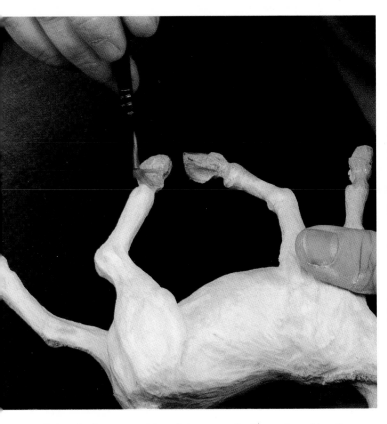

Paint the hooves and brush it out on the lower legs, blending with the white as you go higher.

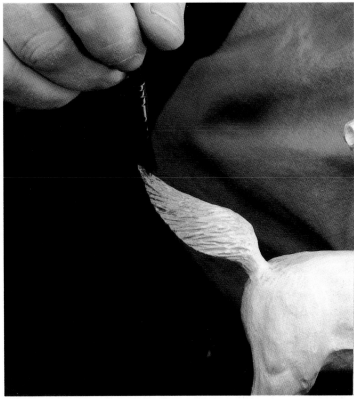

Dry brush a little black on the tail...

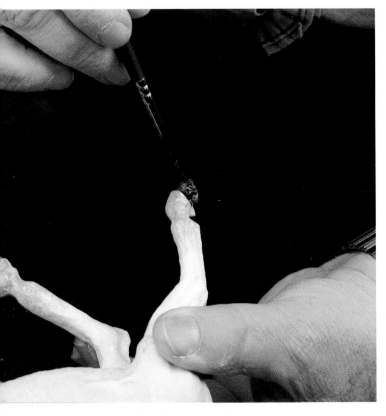

Apply black to the hoof.

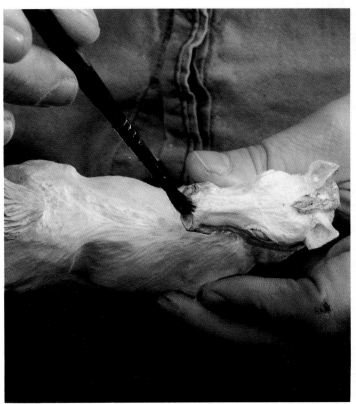

and the muzzle.

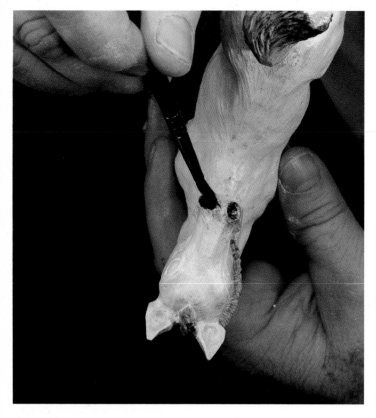

A little heavier application of black in the nostrils.

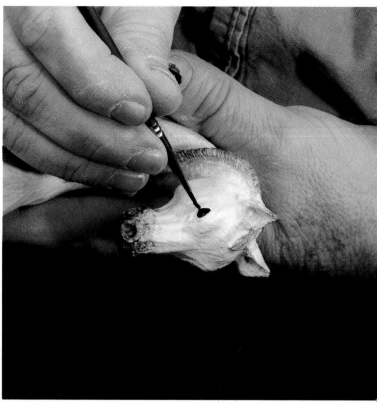

Paint the eyeballs with thick black paint.

and around the mouth.

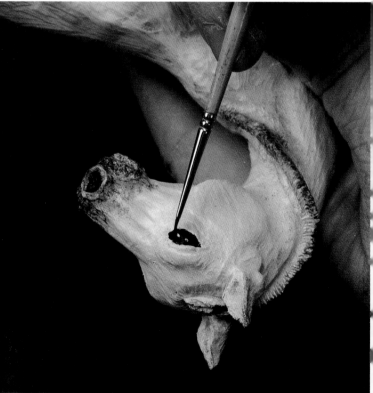

Apply a speck of white to the eyes.

Ready for mounting.

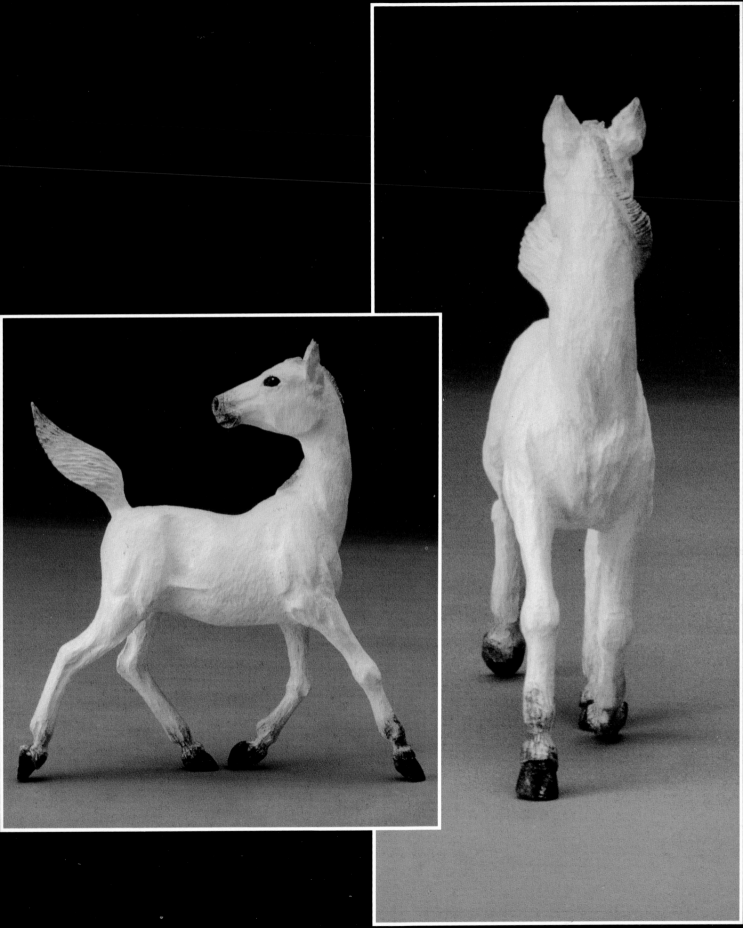

Reduced to 75%.
Enlarge 129% for full size.

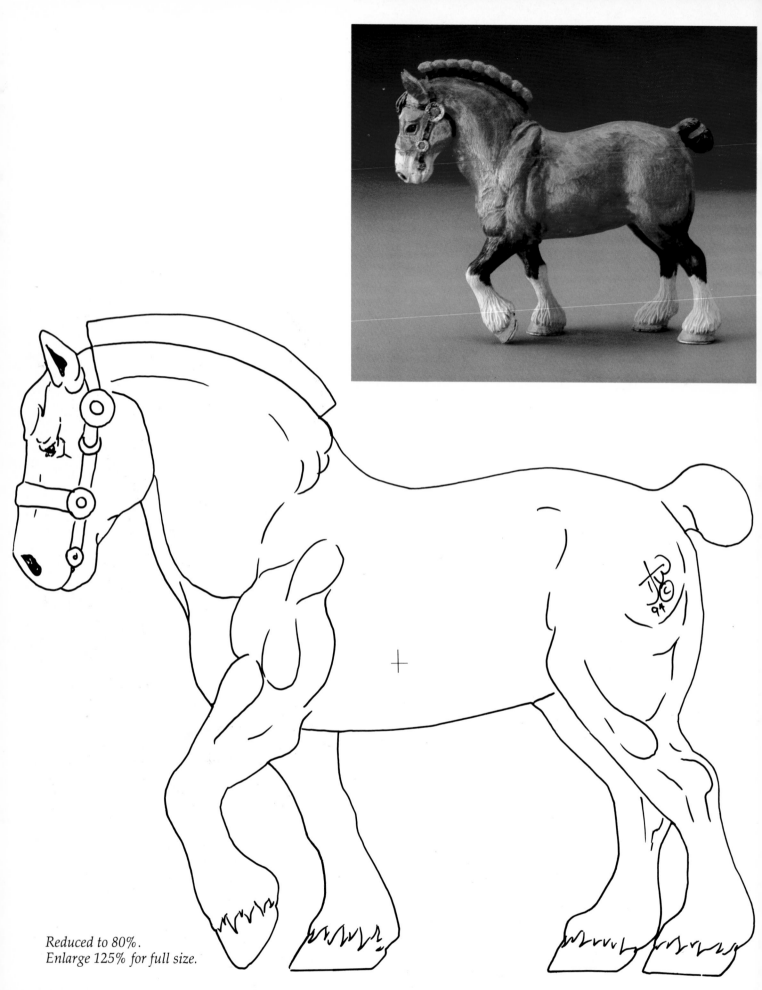

Reduced to 80%.
Enlarge 125% for full size.

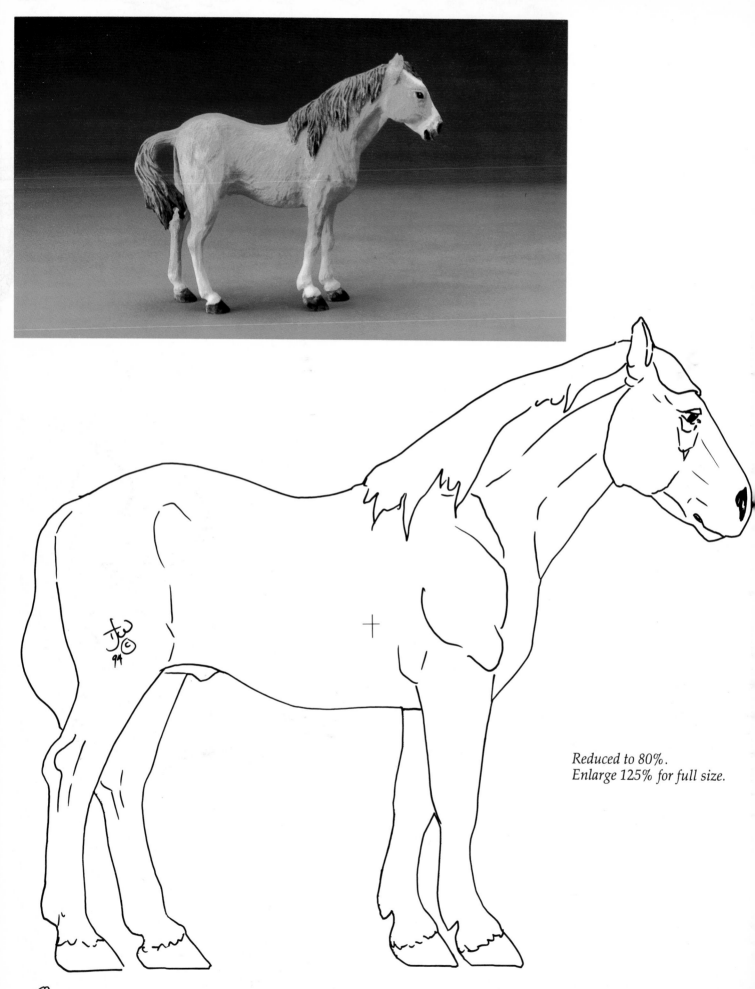

Reduced to 80%.
Enlarge 125% for full size.